THOUGHTS IN
SOLITUDE

BY THOMAS MERTON

THOMAS MERTON

THOUGHTS IN

SOLITUDE

FARRAR • STRAUS • GIROUX / NEW YORK

Farrar, Straus and Giroux
19 Union Square West, New York 10003

AUTHOR'S NOTE

Those who have been indulgent enough to find something that interested them in *Seeds of Contemplation* and *No Man Is an Island* may perhaps be capable of taking some pleasure in these reflections which, if they have any value at all, have the merit of saying here and there some of the things the author most wanted to say to himself and to those who might be inclined to agree with him. And this is especially true of the second part, on "The Love of Solitude." Those who know Max Picard's stimulating pages in *The World of Silence* will recognize the inspiration of the Swiss philosopher in many of these meditations.

CONTENTS

PREFACE

The notes found in these pages were written in 1953 and 1954 at times when the author, by the grace of God and the favor of his Superiors, was able to enjoy special opportunities for solitude and meditation. Hence the title. This does not imply that the notes are subjective or autobiographical. They are in no way intended as an account of spiritual adventures. As far as the writer is concerned, there was no adventure to write about, and if there had been, it would not have been confided to paper in any case. These are simply thoughts on the contemplative life, fundamental intuitions which seemed, at the time, to have a basic importance.

Here, of course, a qualification is demanded.

It is quite likely that the intuitions which seem to be most vital to the writer will not have much importance for others, who do not have the same kind of vocation. So in that sense the book is, after all, quite personal. Sometimes the statements made are rather general, sometimes they are observations made *en passant* and which border on the commonplace. Nowhere will these notes be found esoteric. But in the main these reflections on man's solitude before God, man's dialogue with God in silence, and the interrelation of our personal solitudes with one another, are for the writer essential to his own peculiar way of life. It may also be said, in parentheses, that this peculiar way is not necessarily the ideal of the Religious Order to which the writer happens to belong. It is, for all that, a substantially monastic ideal.

It need hardly be added that much water has passed under the writer's own private bridge since these notes were written, and the lines of thought that are found here have travelled in various unexpected directions in the intervening years.

In an age when totalitarianism has striven, in every way, to devaluate and degrade the human person, we hope it is right to demand a hearing for any and every sane reaction in the favor of man's inalienable solitude and his interior freedom. The murderous din of our materialism cannot be allowed to silence the independent voices which will never cease to speak: whether they be the voices of Christian Saints, or the voices of Oriental sages like Lao-Tse or the Zen Masters, or the voices of men like Thoreau or Martin Buber, or Max Picard. It is all very well to insist that man is a "social animal"—the fact is obvious enough. But that is no justification for making him a mere cog in a totalitarian machine—or in a religious one either, for that matter.

In actual fact, society depends for its existence on the inviolable personal solitude of its members. Society, to merit its name, must be made up not of numbers, or mechanical units, but of persons. To be a person implies responsibility and freedom, and both these imply a certain interior solitude, a sense of personal integrity, a sense of one's own reality and of one's ability to give himself to society—or to refuse that gift.

When men are merely submerged in a mass of impersonal human beings pushed around by automatic forces, they lose their true humanity, their integrity, their ability to love, their capacity for self-determination. When society is made up of men who know no interior solitude it can no longer be held together by love: and consequently it is held together by a violent and abusive authority. But when men are violently deprived of the solitude and freedom which are their due, the society in which they live becomes putrid, it festers with servility, resentment and hate.

No amount of technological progress will cure the hatred that eats away the vitals of materialistic society like a spiritual cancer. The only cure is, and must always be, spiritual. There is not much use talking to men about God and love if they are not able to listen. The ears with which one hears the message of the Gospel are hidden in man's heart, and these ears do not hear anything unless they are favored with a certain interior solitude and silence.

In other words, since faith is a matter of freedom and self-determination—the free receiving of a freely given gift of grace—man cannot assent to a spiritual message as long as his mind and heart are enslaved by automatism. He will always remain so enslaved as long as he is submerged in a mass of other automatons, without individuality and without their rightful integrity as persons.

What is said here about solitude is not just a recipe for hermits. It has a bearing on the whole future of man and of his world: and especially, of course, on the future of his religion.

PART ONE

ASPECTS OF THE SPIRITUAL LIFE

I

There is no greater disaster in the spiritual life than to be immersed in unreality, for life is maintained and nourished in us by our vital relation with realities outside and above us. When our life feeds on unreality, it must starve. It must therefore die. There is no greater misery than to mistake this fruitless death for the true, fruitful and sacrificial "death" by which we enter into life.

The death by which we enter into life is not an escape from reality but a complete gift of ourselves which involves a total commitment to reality. It begins by renouncing the illusory reality which created things acquire when they are seen only in their relation to our own selfish interests.

Before we can see that created things (especially material) are unreal, we must see clearly that they are real.

For the "unreality" of material things is only relative to the *greater* reality of spiritual things.

We begin our renouncement of creatures by standing back from them and looking at them as they are in themselves. In so doing we penetrate their reality, their actuality, their truth, which cannot be discovered until we get them outside ourselves and stand back so that they are seen in perspective. We cannot see things in perspective until we cease to hug them to our own bosom. When we let go of them we begin to appreciate them as they really are. Only then can we begin to see God in them. Not until we find Him in them, can we start on the road of dark contemplation at whose end we shall be able to find them in Him.

The Desert Fathers believed that the wilderness had been created as supremely valuable in the eyes of God precisely because it had no value to men. The wasteland was the land that could never be wasted by men because it offered them nothing. There was nothing to attract them. There was nothing to exploit. The desert was the region in which the Chosen People had wandered for forty years, cared for by God alone. They could have reached the Promised Land in a few months if they had travelled directly to it. God's plan was that they should learn to love Him in the wilderness and that they should always look back upon the time in the desert as the idyllic time of their life with Him alone.

The desert was created simply to be itself, not to be transformed by men into something else. So too the mountain and the sea. The desert is therefore the logical dwelling place for the man who seeks to be nothing but himself—that is to say, a creature solitary and poor and dependent upon no one but God, with no great project standing between himself and his Creator.

This is, at least, the theory. But there is another factor that enters in. First, the desert is the country of madness. Second, it is the refuge of the devil, thrown out into the "wilderness of upper Egypt" to "wander in dry places." Thirst drives man mad, and the devil himself is mad with a kind of thirst for his own lost excellence—lost because he has immured himself in it and closed out everything else.

So the man who wanders into the desert to be himself must take care that he does not go mad and become the servant of the one who dwells there in a sterile paradise of emptiness and rage.

Yet look at the deserts today. What are they? The birthplace of a new and terrible creation, the testing-ground of the power by which man seeks to un-create what God has blessed. Today, in the century of man's greatest technological achievement, the wilderness at last comes into its own. Man no longer needs God, and he can live in the desert on his own resources. He can build there his fantastic, protected cities of withdrawal and experimentation and vice. The glittering towns that spring up overnight in the desert are no longer images of the City of God, coming down from heaven to enlighten the world with the vision of peace. They are not even replicas of the great tower of Babel that once rose up in the desert of Senaar, that man "might make his name famous and reach even unto heaven" (Genesis 11:4). They are brilliant and sordid smiles of the devil upon the face of the wilderness, cities of secrecy where each man spies on his brother, cities through whose veins money runs like artificial blood, and from whose womb will come the last and greatest instrument of destruction.

Can we watch the growth of these cities and not do something to purify our own hearts? When man and his money and machines move out into the desert, and dwell there, not fighting the devil as Christ did, but believing in his promises of power and wealth, and adoring his angelic wisdom, then the desert itself moves everywhere. Everywhere is desert. Everywhere is solitude in which man must do penance and fight the adversary and purify his own heart in the grace of God.

The desert is the home of despair. And despair, now, is everywhere. Let us not think that our interior solitude consists in the acceptance of defeat. We cannot escape anything by consenting tacitly to be defeated. Despair is an abyss without bottom. Do not think to close it by consenting to it and trying to forget you have consented.

This, then, is our desert: to live facing despair, but not to consent. To trample it down under hope in the Cross. To wage war against despair unceasingly. That war is our wilderness. If we wage it courageously, we will find Christ at our side. If we cannot face it, we will never find Him.

II

Temperament does not predestine one man to sanctity and another to reprobation. All temperaments can serve as the material for ruin or for salvation. We must learn to see that our temperament is a gift of God, a talent with which we must trade until He comes. It does not matter how poor or how difficult a temperament we may be endowed with. If we make good use of what we have, if we make it serve our good desires, we can do better than another who merely serves his temperament instead of making it serve him.

St. Thomas says [I-II, Q.34,a.4] that a man is good when his will takes joy in what is good, evil when his will takes joy in what is evil. He is virtuous when he finds happiness in a virtuous life, sinful when he takes pleasure in a sinful life. Hence the things that we love tell us what we are.

A man is known, then, by his end. He is also known by his beginning. And if you wish to know him as he is at any given moment, find how far he is from his beginning and how near to his end. Hence, too, the man who sins in spite of himself but does not love his sin, is not a sinner in the full sense of the word.

The good man comes from God and returns to Him. He starts with the gift of being and with the capacities God has given him. He reaches the age of reason and begins to make choices. The character of his choices is already to a great extent influenced by what has happened to him in the first years of his life, and by the temperament with which he is born. It will continue to be influenced by the actions of others around him, by the events of the world in which he lives, by the character of his society. Nevertheless it remains fundamentally free.

But human freedom does not act in a moral vacuum. Nor is it necessary to produce such a vacuum in order to guarantee the freedom of our activity. Coercion from outside, strong temperamental inclinations and passions within ourselves, do nothing to affect the essence of our freedom. They simply define its action by imposing certain limits on it. They give it a peculiar character of its own.

A temperamentally angry man may be more inclined to anger than another. But as long as he remains sane he is still free not to be angry. His inclination to anger is simply a force in his character which can be turned to good or evil, according to his desires. If he desires what is evil, his temper will become a weapon of evil against other men and even against his own soul. If he desires what is good his temper can become the controlled instrument for fighting the evil that is in himself and helping other men to overcome the obstacles which they meet in the world. He remains free to desire either good or evil.

. . .

It would be absurd to suppose that because emotion sometimes interferes with reason, that it therefore has no place in the spiritual life. Christianity is not stoicism. The Cross does not sanctify us by destroying human feeling. Detachment is not insensibility. Too many ascetics fail to become great saints precisely because their rules and ascetic practices have merely deadened their humanity instead of setting it free to develop richly, in all its capacities, under the influence of grace.

A saint is a perfect man. He is a temple of the Holy Ghost. He reproduces, in his own individual way, something of the balance and perfection and order that we find in the Human character of Jesus. The soul of Jesus, hypostatically united to the Word of God, enjoyed at the same time and without conflict the Clear Vision of God and the most common and simple and intimate of our human emotions—affection, pity and sorrow, happiness, pleasure, or grief; indignation and wonder; weariness, anxiety and fear; consolation and peace.

If we are without human feelings we cannot love God in the way in which we are meant to love Him—as men. If we do not respond to human affection we cannot be loved by God in the way in which He has willed to love us—with the Heart of the Man, Jesus Who is God, the Son of God, and the anointed Christ.

The ascetical life, therefore, must be begun and carried on with a supreme respect for temperament, character, and emotion, and for everything that makes us human. These too are integral elements in personality and therefore in sanctity—because a saint is one whom God's love has fully developed into a person in the likeness of his Creator.

The control of emotion by self-denial tends to mature and perfect our human sensibility. Ascetic discipline does not spare our sensibility: for if it does so, it fails in its duty. If we really deny ourselves, our self-denial will sometimes even deprive us of things we really need. Therefore we will feel the need of them.

We must suffer. But the attack of mortification upon sense, sensibility, imagination, judgment and will is intended to enrich and purify them all. Our five senses are dulled by inordinate pleasure. Penance makes them keen, gives them back their natural vitality, and more. Penance clears the eye of conscience and of reason. It helps us think clearly, judge sanely. It strengthens the action of our will. And Penance also tones up the quality of emotion; it is the lack of self-denial and self-discipline that explains the mediocrity of so much devotional art, so much pious writing, so much sentimental prayer, so many religious lives.

Some men turn away from all this cheap emotion with a kind of heroic despair, and seek God in a desert where the emotions can find nothing to sustain them. But this too can be an error. For if our emotions really die in the desert, our humanity dies with them. We must return from the desert like Jesus or St. John, with our capacity for feeling expanded and deepened, strengthened against the appeals of falsity, warned against temptation, great, noble and pure.

III

Spiritual life is not mental life. It is not thought alone. Nor is it, of course, a life of sensation, a life of feeling—"feeling" and experiencing the things of the spirit, and the things of God.

Nor does the spiritual life exclude thought and feeling. It needs both. It is not just a life concentrated at the "high point" of the soul, a life from which the mind and the imagination and the body are excluded. If it were so, few people could lead it. And again, if that were the spiritual life, it would not be a life at all. If man is to live, he must be all alive, body, soul, mind, heart, spirit. Everything must be elevated and transformed by the action of God, in love and faith.

Useless to try to meditate merely by "think-ing"—still worse to meditate by stringing words together, reviewing an army of platitudes.

A purely mental life may be destructive if it leads us to substitute thought for life and ideas for actions. The activity proper to man is not purely mental because man is not just a disem-bodied mind. Our destiny is to live out what we think, because unless we live what we know, we do not even know it. It is only by making our knowledge part of ourselves, through action, that we enter into the reality that is signified by our concepts.

To live as a rational animal does not mean to think as a man and to live as an animal. We must both think and live as men. Illusion to try to live as if the two abstract parts of our being (rationality and animality) existed separately in fact as two different concrete realities. We are one, body and soul, and unless we live as a unity we must die.

Living is not thinking. Thought is formed and guided by objective reality outside us. Living is the constant adjustment of thought to life and life to thought in such a way that we are always growing, always experiencing new things in the old and old things in the new. Thus life is always new.

IV

The phrase self-conquest can come to sound odious because very often it can mean not the conquest of ourselves but a conquest *by* ourselves. A victory we have won by our own power. Over what? Precisely over what is other than ourself.

Real self-conquest is the conquest of ourselves not by ourselves but by the Holy Spirit. Self-conquest is really self-surrender.

Yet before we can surrender ourselves we must become ourselves. For no one can give up what he does not possess.

More precisely—we have to have enough mastery of ourselves to renounce our own will into the hands of Christ—so that He may conquer what we cannot reach by our own efforts.

In order to gain possession of ourselves, we have to have some confidence, some hope of victory. And in order to keep that hope alive we must usually have some taste of victory. We must know what victory is and like it better than defeat.

There is no hope for the man who struggles to obtain a virtue in the abstract—a quality of which he has no experience. He will never efficaciously prefer the virtue to the opposite vice, no matter how much he may seem to despise the latter.

Everybody has an instinctive desire to do good things and avoid evil. But that desire is sterile as long as we have no experience of what it means to be good.

(The desire for virtue is frustrated in many men of good will by the distaste they instinctively feel for the false virtues of those who are supposed to be holy. Sinners have a very keen eye for false virtues and a very exacting idea of what virtue should be in a good man. If in the men who are supposed to be good they only see a "virtue" which is effectively less vital and less interesting than their own vices they will conclude that virtue has no meaning, and will cling to what they have although they hate it.)

But what if we have no virtue? How can we then experience it? The grace of God, through Christ Our Lord, produces in us a desire for virtue which is an anticipated experience of that virtue. He makes us capable of "liking" virtue before we fully possess it.

Grace, which is charity, contains in itself all virtues in a hidden and potential manner, like the leaves and the branches of the oak hidden in the meat of an acorn. To be an acorn is to have a taste for being an oak tree. Habitual grace brings with it all the Christian virtues in their seed.

Actual graces move us to actualize these hidden powers and to realize what they mean:— Christ acting in us.

The pleasure of a good act is something to be remembered—not in order to feed our complacency but in order to remind us that virtuous actions are not only possible and valuable, but that they can become *easier* and more delightful and more fruitful than the acts of vice which oppose and frustrate them.

A false humility should not rob us of the pleasure of conquest which is due to us and necessary for our spiritual life, especially in the beginning.

It is true that later on we may be left with faults we cannot conquer—in order that we may have the humility to fight against a seemingly unbeatable opponent, without any of the satisfaction of victory. For we may be asked to renounce even the pleasure we take in doing good things in order to make sure that we do them for something more than pleasure. But before we can renounce that pleasure, we must first acquire it. In the beginning, the pleasure of self-conquest is necessary. Let us not be afraid to desire it.

V

Laziness and cowardice are two of the greatest enemies of the spiritual life. And they are most dangerous of all when they mask as "discretion." This illusion would not be so fatal if discretion itself were not one of the most important virtues of a spiritual man. Indeed, it is discretion itself that must teach us the difference between cowardice and discretion. *If thine eye be simple . . . but if the light which is in thee be darkness . . .*

Discretion tells us what God wants of us and what He does not want of us. In telling us this, it shows us our obligation to correspond with the inspirations of grace and to obey all the other indications of God's will.

Laziness and cowardice put our own present comfort before the love of God. They fear the uncertainty of the future because they place no trust in God.

Discretion warns us against wasted effort: but for the coward all effort is wasted effort. Discretion shows us where effort is wasted and when it is obligatory.

Laziness flies from all risk. Discretion flies from useless risk: but urges us on to take the risks that faith and the grace of God demand of us. For when Jesus said the kingdom of heaven was to be won by violence, He meant that it could only be bought at the price of certain risks.

And sooner or later, if we follow Christ we have to risk everything in order to gain everything. We have to gamble on the invisible and risk all that we can see and taste and feel. But we know the risk is worth it, because there is nothing more insecure than the transient world. *For this world as we see it is passing away* (1 Corinthians 7:31).

Without courage we can never attain to true simplicity. Cowardice keeps us "double minded" —hesitating between the world and God. In this hesitation, there is no true faith—faith remains an opinion. We are never certain, because we never quite give in to the authority of an invisible God. This hesitation is the death of hope. We never let go of those visible supports which, we well know, must one day surely fail us. And this hesitation makes true prayer impossible—it never quite dares to ask for anything, or if it asks, it is so uncertain of being heard that in the very act of asking, it surreptitiously seeks by human prudence to construct a make-shift answer (cf James 1:5–8).

What is the use of praying if at the very moment of prayer, we have so little confidence in God that we are busy planning our own kind of answer to our prayer?

VI

There is no true spiritual life outside the love of Christ. We have a spiritual life only because we are loved by Him. The spiritual life consists in receiving the gift of the Holy Spirit and His charity, because the Sacred Heart of Jesus has willed, in His love, that we should live by His Spirit—the same Spirit which proceeds from the Word and from the Father, and Who is Jesus' love for the Father.

If we know how great is the love of Jesus for us we will never be afraid to go to Him in all our poverty, all our weakness, all our spiritual wretchedness and infirmity. Indeed, when we understand the true nature of His love for us, we will prefer to come to Him poor and helpless. We will never be ashamed of our distress. Distress is to our advantage when we have nothing to seek but mercy. We can be glad of our helplessness when we really believe that His power is made perfect in our infirmity.

The surest sign that we have received a spiritual understanding of God's love for us is the appreciation of our own poverty in the light of His infinite mercy.

We must love our own poverty as Jesus loves it. It is so valuable to Him that He died on the Cross to present our poverty to His Father, and endow us with the riches of His own infinite mercy.

We must love the poverty of others as Jesus loves it. We must see them with the eyes of His own compassion. But we cannot have true compassion on others unless we are willing to accept pity and receive forgiveness for our own sins.

We do not really know how to forgive until we know what it is to be forgiven. Therefore we should be glad that we can be forgiven by our brothers. It is our forgiveness of one another that makes the love of Jesus for us manifest in our lives, for in forgiving one another we act towards one another as He has acted towards us.

VII

A Christian is a man who lives completely out of himself in Christ—he lives in the faith of his Redemption, in the love of his Redeemer, loving us for whom He died. He lives, above all, in the hope of a world to come.

Hope is the secret of true asceticism. It denies our own judgments and desires and rejects the world in its present state, not because either we or the world are evil, but because we are not in a condition to make the best use of our own or of the world's goodness. But we rejoice in hope. We enjoy created things in hope. We enjoy them not as they are in themselves but as they are in Christ—full of promise. For the goodness of all things is a witness to the goodness of God and

His goodness is a guarantee of His fidelity to His promises. He has promised us a new heaven and a new earth, a risen life in Christ. All self-denial that is not entirely suspended from His promise is something less than Christian.

My Lord, I have no hope but in Your Cross. You, by Your humility, and sufferings and death, have delivered me from all vain hope. You have killed the vanity of the present life in Yourself, and have given me all that is eternal in rising from the dead.

Why should I want to be rich, when You were poor? Why should I desire to be famous and powerful in the eyes of men, when the sons of those who exalted the false prophets and stoned the true rejected You and nailed You to the Cross? Why should I cherish in my heart a hope that devours me—the hope for perfect happiness in this life—when such hope, doomed to frustration, is nothing but despair?

My hope is in what the eye has never seen. Therefore, let me not trust in visible rewards. My hope is in what the heart of man cannot feel. Therefore let me not trust in the feelings of my heart. My hope is in what the hand of man has never touched. Do not let me trust what I can grasp between my fingers. Death will loosen my grasp and my vain hope will be gone.

Let my trust be in Your mercy, not in myself. Let my hope be in Your love, not in health, or strength, or ability or human resources.

If I trust You, everything else will become, for me, strength, health, and support. Everything will bring me to heaven. If I do not trust You, everything will be my destruction.

 VIII

All sin is a punishment for the primal sin of not knowing God. That is to say all sin is a punishment for ingratitude. For as St. Paul says (Romans 1:21), the Gentiles, who "knew" God, did not *know* Him because they were not grateful for the knowledge of Him. They did not know Him because their knowledge did not gladden them with His love. For if we do not love Him we show that we do not know Him. He is love. *Deus caritas est.*

Our knowledge of God is perfected by gratitude: we are thankful and rejoice in the experience of the truth that He is love.

The Eucharist—the Sacrifice of praise and thanksgiving—is a burning hearth of the knowledge of God for in the Sacrifice Jesus, giving thanks to the Father, offers and immolates Himself entirely for His Father's glory and to save us from our sins. If we do not "know" Him in His sacrifice, how can it avail for us? "The knowledge of God is *more than holocausts*" (Osee 6:6). We do not know Him unless we are grateful, and praise the Father with Him.

There is no neutrality between gratitude and ingratitude. Those who are not grateful soon begin to complain of everything. Those who do not love, hate. In the spiritual life there is no such thing as an indifference to love or hate. That is why tepidity (which seems to be indifferent) is so detestable. It is hate disguised as love.

Tepidity, in which the soul is neither "hot or cold"—neither frankly loves nor frankly hates—is a state in which one rejects God and rejects the will of God while maintaining an exterior pretense of loving Him in order to keep out of trouble and save one's supposed self-respect. It is the condition that is soon arrived at by those who are habitually ungrateful for the graces of

God. A man who truly responds to the goodness of God, and acknowledges all that he has received, cannot possibly be a half-hearted Christian. True gratitude and hypocrisy cannot exist together. They are totally incompatible. Gratitude of itself makes us sincere—or if it does not, then it is not true gratitude.

Gratitude, though, is more than a mental exercise, more than a formula of words. We cannot be satisfied to make a mental note of things which God has done for us and then perfunctorily thank Him for favors received.

To be grateful is to recognize the Love of God in everything He has given us—and He has given us everything. Every breath we draw is a gift of His love, every moment of existence is a grace, for it brings with it immense graces from Him. Gratitude therefore takes nothing for granted, is never unresponsive, is constantly awakening to new wonder and to praise of the goodness of God. For the grateful man knows that God is good, not by hearsay but by experience. And that is what makes all the difference.

ℐ IX

What does it mean to know and experience my own "nothingness"?

It is not enough to turn away in disgust from my illusions and faults and mistakes, to separate myself from them as if they were not, and as if I were someone other than myself. This kind of self-annihilation is only a worse illusion, it is a pretended humility which, by saying "I am nothing" I mean in effect "I wish I were not what I am."

This can flow from an experience of our deficiencies and of our helplessness, but it does not produce any peace in us. To really know our "nothingness" we must also love it. And we cannot love it unless we see that it is good. And we cannot see that it is good unless we accept it.

A supernatural experience of our contingency is a humility which loves and prizes above all else our state of moral and metaphysical helplessness before God.

To love our "nothingness" in this way, we must repudiate nothing that is our own, nothing that we have, nothing that we are. We must see and admit that it is all ours and that it is all good: good in its positive entity since it comes from God: good in our deficiency, since our helplessness, even our moral misery, our spiritual, attracts to us the mercy of God.

To love our nothingness we must love everything in us that the proud man loves when he loves himself. But we must love it all for exactly the opposite reason.

To love our nothingness we must love *ourselves*.

But the proud man loves himself because he thinks he is worthy of love and respect and veneration for his own sake. Because he thinks he *must* be loved by God and man. Because he thinks he is more worthy to be honored and loved and reverenced than all other men.

The humble man also loves himself, and seeks to be loved and honored, not because love and honor are *due to him* but because they are *not due to him*. He seeks to be loved by the mercy of God. He begs to be loved and helped by the liberality of his fellow men. Knowing that he has nothing he also knows that he *needs* everything and he is not afraid to beg for what he needs and to get it where he can.

The proud man loves his own illusion and self-sufficiency. The spiritually poor man loves his very insufficiency. The proud man claims honor for having what no one else has. The humble man begs for a share in what everybody else has received. He too desires to be filled to overflowing with the kindness and mercy of God.

X

The spiritual life is first of all a *life*.

It is not merely something to be known and studied, it is to be lived. Like all life, it grows sick and dies when it is uprooted from its proper element. Grace is engrafted on our nature and the whole man is sanctified by the presence and action of the Holy Spirit. The spiritual life is not, therefore, a life entirely uprooted from man's human condition and transplanted into the realm of the angels. We live as spiritual men when we live as men seeking God. If we are to become spiritual, we must remain men. And if there were not evidence of this everywhere in theology, the Mystery of the Incarnation itself would be ample proof of it. Why did Christ become Man if not to save men by uniting them mystically with God through His own Sacred Humanity? Jesus lived the ordinary life of the men of His time, in order to sanctify the ordinary lives of men of all time. If we want to be spiritual, then, let us first of all live our lives. Let us not fear the responsibilities and the inevitable distractions of the work appointed for us by the will of God. Let us embrace reality and thus find ourselves immersed in the life-giving will and wisdom of God which surrounds us everywhere.

First, let us be sure that we know what we are doing. Faith alone can give us the light to see that God's will is to be found in our everyday life. Without this light, we cannot see to make the right decisions. Without this certitude we cannot have supernatural confidence and peace. We stumble and fall constantly even when we are most enlightened. But when we are in true spiritual darkness, we do not even know that we have fallen.

To keep ourselves spiritually alive we must

constantly renew our faith. We are like pilots of fogbound steamers, peering into the gloom in front of us, listening for the sounds of other ships, and we can only reach our harbor if we keep alert. The spiritual life is, then, first of all a matter of keeping awake. We must not lose our sensitivity to spiritual inspirations. We must always be able to respond to the slightest warnings that speak, as though by a hidden instinct, in the depth of the soul that is spiritually alive.

Meditation is one of the ways in which the spiritual man keeps himself awake. It is not really a paradox that it is precisely in meditation that most aspirants for religious perfection grow dull and fall asleep. Meditative prayer is a stern discipline, and one which cannot be learned by violence. It requires unending courage and perseverance, and those who are not willing to work at it patiently will finally end in compromise. Here, as elsewhere, compromise is only another name for failure.

To meditate is to think. And yet successful meditation is much more than reasoning or thinking. It is much more than "affections," much more than a series of prepared "acts" which one goes through.

In meditative prayer, one thinks and speaks not only with his mind and lips, but in a certain sense with his *whole being*. Prayer is then not just a formula of words, or a series of desires springing up in the heart—it is the orientation of our whole body, mind and spirit to God in silence, attention, and adoration. All good meditative prayer is a *conversion of our entire self to God*.

One cannot then enter into meditation, in this sense, without a kind of inner upheaval. By upheaval I do not mean a disturbance, but a breaking out of routine, a liberation of the heart from the cares and preoccupations of one's daily business. The reason why so few people apply themselves seriously to mental prayer is precisely that this inner upheaval is necessary, and they are usually incapable of the effort required to make it. It may be that they lack generosity, and it may also be that they lack direction and experience, and go about it the wrong way. They disturb themselves, they throw themselves into agitation by the violent efforts they make to get recollected, and finally they end in hopelessness. They compromise, in the end, by a series of frustrated routines which help them to pass the time, or else they relax into a state of semicoma which, they hope, can be justified by the name of contemplation.

Every spiritual director knows that it is a difficult and subtle matter to determine just what is the borderline between interior idleness and the faint, unperceived beginnings of passive contemplation. But in practice, at the present time, there has been quite enough said about passive contemplation to give lazy people a chance to claim the privilege of "praying by doing nothing."

There is no such thing as a prayer in which "nothing is done" or "nothing happens," although there may well be a prayer in which nothing is perceived or felt or thought.

All real interior prayer, no matter how simple

it may be, requires the conversion of our whole self to God, and until this has been achieved—either actively by our own efforts or passively by the action of the Holy Spirit—we do not enter into "contemplation" and we cannot safely relax our efforts to establish contact with God.

If we try to contemplate God without having turned the face of our inner self entirely in His direction, we will end up inevitably by contemplating ourselves, and we will perhaps plunge into the abyss of warm darkness which is our own sensible nature. That is not a darkness in which one can safely remain passive.

On the other hand, if we depend too much on our imagination and emotions, we will not turn ourselves to God but will plunge into a riot of images and fabricate for ourselves our own home-made religious experience, and this too is perilous.

The "turning" of our whole self to God can be achieved only by deep and sincere and simple faith, enlivened by a hope which knows that contact with God is possible, and love which desires above all things to do His will.

Sometimes, meditation is nothing but an unsuccessful struggle to turn ourselves to God, to seek His Face by faith. Any number of things beyond our control may make it morally impossible for one to meditate effectively. In that case, faith and good will are sufficient. If one has made a really sincere and honest effort to turn himself to God and cannot seem to get his wits together at all, then the attempt will have to count as a meditation. This means that God, in His mercy, accepts our unsuccessful efforts in the place of a real meditation. Sometimes it happens that this interior helplessness is a sign of real progress in the interior life—for it makes us depend more completely and peacefully on the mercy of God.

If we can, by God's grace, turn ourselves entirely to Him, and put aside everything else in order to speak with Him and worship Him, this does not mean that we can always imagine Him or feel His presence. Neither imagination nor feeling are required for a full conversion of our whole being to God. Nor is intense concentration on an "idea" of God especially desirable.

Hard as it is to convey in human language, there is a very real and very recognizable (but almost entirely undefinable) Presence of God, in which we confront Him in prayer knowing Him by Whom we are known, aware of Him Who is aware of us, loving Him by Whom we know ourselves to be loved. Present to ourselves in the fulness of our own personality, we are present to Him Who is infinite in His Being, His Otherness, His Self-hood. It is not a vision face to face, but a certain presence of self to Self in which, with the reverent attention of our whole being, we know Him in Whom all things have their being. The "eye" which opens to His presence is in the very center of our humility, in the very heart of our freedom, in the very depths of our spiritual nature. Meditation is the opening of this eye.

❧ XI

Nourished by the Sacraments and formed by the prayer and teaching of the Church, we need seek nothing but the particular place willed for us by God within the Church. When we find that place, our life and our prayer both at once become extremely simple.

Then we discover what the spiritual life really is. It is not a matter of doing one good work rather than another, of living in one place rather than in another, of praying in one way rather than in another.

It is not a matter of any special psychological effect in our own soul. It is the silence of our whole being in compunction and adoration before God, in the habitual realization that He is everything and we are nothing, that He is the Center to which all things tend, and to Whom all our actions must be directed. That our life and strength proceed from Him, that both in life and in death we depend entirely on Him, that the whole course of our life is foreknown by Him and falls into the plan of His wise and merciful Providence; that it is absurd to live as though without Him, for ourselves, by ourselves; that all our plans and spiritual ambitions are useless unless they come from Him and end in Him and that, in the end, the only thing that matters is His glory.

We ruin our life of prayer if we are constantly examining our prayer and seeking the fruit of prayer in a peace that is nothing more than a psychological process. The only thing to seek in contemplative prayer is God; and we seek Him successfully when we realize that we cannot find Him unless He shows Himself to us, and yet at the same time that He would not have inspired us to seek Him unless we had already found Him.

The more we are content with our own poverty, the closer we are to God, for then we accept our poverty in peace, expecting nothing from ourselves and everything from God.

Poverty is the door to freedom, not because we remain imprisoned in the anxiety and constraint which poverty of itself implies, but because, finding nothing in ourselves that is a source of hope, we know there is nothing in ourselves worth defending. There is nothing special in ourselves to love. We go out of ourselves therefore and rest in Him in Whom alone is our hope.

There is a stage in the spiritual life in which we find God in ourselves—this presence is a created effect of His love. It is a gift of His, to us. It remains in us. All the gifts of God are good. But if we rest in them, rather than in Him, they lose their goodness for us. So with this gift also.

When the right time comes for us to go on to other things, God withdraws the sense of His presence, in order to strengthen our faith. After that it is useless to seek Him through the medium of any psychological effect. Useless to look for any sense of Him in our hearts. The time has come when we must go out of ourselves and above ourselves and find Him no longer within us but outside us and above us. This we do first by arid faith, by a hope that burns like hot coals under the ashes of our poverty. We seek Him also by humble charity, in service of our brothers. Then, when God wills, He raises us up to Himself in simplicity.

What is the use of knowing our weakness if we do not implore God to sustain us with His power? What is the value of recognizing our poverty if we never use it to entreat His mercy? It is bad enough to be complacent in the thought that we have virtue, but worse to rest in careless inertia when we are conscious of our weakness and of our sins. The value of our weakness and of our poverty is that they are the earth in which God sows the seed of desire. And no matter how abandoned we may seem to be, the confident desire to love Him in spite of our abject misery is the sign of His presence and the pledge of our salvation.

☞ XII

If you want to have a spiritual life you must unify your life. A life is either all spiritual or not spiritual at all. No man can serve two masters. Your life is shaped by the end you live for. You are made in the image of what you desire.

To unify your life, unify your desires. To spiritualize your life, spiritualize your desires. To spiritualize your desires, desire to be without desire.

To live in the spirit is to live for a God in Whom we believe, but Whom we cannot see. To desire this is therefore to renounce the desire of all that can be seen. To possess Him Who cannot be understood is to renounce all that can be understood. To rest in Him Who is beyond all created rest, we renounce the desire to rest in created things.

By renouncing the world we conquer the world, rise above its multiplicity and recapitulate it in the simplicity of a love which finds all things in God.

This is what Jesus meant when He said that any one who would save his life will lose it, and he who would lose his life, for the sake of God, would save it.

The 28th chapter of Job (also of Baruch 3) tells us that the wisdom of God is hidden and impossible to find—and yet ends by assuming that it is easily found, for the fear of the Lord is wisdom.

A monk must never look for wisdom outside his vocation. If he does, he will never find wisdom, because for him wisdom is in his vocation. Wisdom is the very life of the monk in his monastery. It is by living his life that the monk finds God, and not by adding something to his life which God has not put there. For wisdom is God Himself, living in us, revealing Himself to us. Life reveals itself to us only in so far as we live it.

The monastic life is full of the mercy of God. Everything the monk does is willed by God and ordered to the glory of God. In doing God's will we receive the mercy of God, because it is only by a gift of His mercy that we can do His will with a pure and supernatural intention. And He gives us this intention as a grace which serves only as a means for us to obtain more grace, and more mercy, by enlarging our capacity to love Him. The greater our capacity to receive His mercy, the greater is our power to give Him glory, for He is glorified only by His own gifts, and He is most glorified by those in whom His mercy has produced the greatest love. "He loves little who has little forgiven him" (Luke 7:47).

XIII

The poorest man in a religious community is not necessarily the one who has the fewest objects assigned to him for his use. Poverty is not merely a matter of not having "things." It is an attitude which leads us to renounce some of the advantages which come from the use of things. A man can possess nothing, but attach great importance to the personal satisfaction and enjoyment he wants to get out of things which are common to all—the chant in choir, the sermons in chapter, the reading in the refectory—free time, other people's time . . .

Often the poorest man in the community is the one who is at everybody else's disposition. He can be used by all and never takes time to do anything special for himself.

Poverty—can bear on things like our opinion, our "style," anything that tends to affirm us as distinct from others, as superior to others in such a way that we take satisfaction in these peculiarities and treat them as "possessions." "Poverty" should not make us peculiar. The eccentric man is not poor in spirit.

Even the ability to help others and to give our time and possessions to them can be "possessed" with attachment if by these actions we are really forcing ourselves on others and obligating them to ourselves. For in that case we are trying to buy them and get possession of them by the favors we do for them.

What one of us, O Lord, can speak of poverty without shame? We who have taken vows of poverty in the monastery: are we really poor? Do we know what it is to love poverty? Have we even stopped to think, for a moment, why poverty is to be loved?

Yet You, O Lord, came into the world to be poor among the poor, because it is easier for a camel to get through the eye of a needle than for a rich man to get into the Kingdom of Heaven. And we, with our vow, we are content with the fact that we legally possess nothing, and that for everything we have, we must ask someone else's permission?

Is this poverty? Can a man who has lost his job and who has no money with which to pay his bills, and who sees his wife and children getting thin, and who feels fear and anger eating out his heart—can he get the things he desperately needs merely by asking for them? Let him try. And yet we, who can have many things we don't need and many more which are scandalous for us to have—we are poor, because we have them with permission!

Poverty means need. To make a vow of poverty and never go without anything, never have to need something without getting it, is to try to mock the Living God.

 XIV

Reading ought to be an act of hommage to the God of all truth. We open our hearts to words that reflect the reality He has created or the greater Reality which He is. It is also an act of humility and reverence towards other men who are the instruments by which God communicated His truth to us.

Reading gives God more glory when we get more out of it, when it is a more deeply vital act not only of our intelligence but of our whole personality, absorbed and refreshed in thought, meditation, prayer, or even in the contemplation of God.

Books can speak to us like God, like men or like the noise of the city we live in. They speak to us like God when they bring us light and peace and fill us with silence. They speak to us like God when we desire never to leave them. They speak to us like men when we desire to hear them again. They speak to us like the noise of the city when they hold us captive by a weariness that tells us nothing, give us no peace, and no support, nothing to remember, and yet will not let us escape.

Books that speak like God speak with too much authority to entertain us. Those that speak like good men hold us by their human charm; we grow by finding ourselves in them. They teach us to know ourselves better by recognizing ourselves in another.

Books that speak like the noise of multitudes reduce us to despair by the sheer weight of their emptiness. They entertain us like the lights of the city streets at night, by hopes they cannot fulfil.

Great though books may be, friends though they may be to us, they are no substitute for persons, they are only means of contact with great persons, with men who had more than their own share of humanity, men who were persons for the whole world and not for themselves alone.

Ideas and words are not the food of the intelligence, but truth. And not an abstract truth that feeds the mind alone. The Truth that a spiritual man seeks is the whole Truth, reality, existence and essence together, something that can be embraced and loved, something that can sustain the homage and the service of our actions: more than a thing: persons, or a Person. Him above all Whose essence is to exist. God.

Christ, the Incarnate Word, is the Book of Life in Whom we read God.

 XV

Humility is a virtue, not a neurosis.

It sets us free to act virtuously, to serve God and to know Him. Therefore true humility can never inhibit any really virtuous action, nor can it prevent us from fulfilling ourselves by doing the will of God.

Humility sets us free to do what is really good, by showing us our *illusions* and withdrawing our will from what was only an *apparent* good.

A humility that freezes our being and frustrates all healthy activity is not humility at all, but a disguised form of pride. It dries up the roots of the spiritual life and makes it impossible for us to give ourselves to God.

Lord, You have taught us to love humility, but we have not learned. We have learned only to love the outward surface of it—the humility that makes a person charming and attractive. We sometimes pause to think about these qualities, and we often pretend that we possess them, and that we have gained them by "practicing humility."

If we were really humble, we would know to what an extent we are liars!

Teach me to bear a humility which shows me, without ceasing, that I am a liar and a fraud and that, even though this is so, I have an obligation to strive after truth, to be as true as I can, even though I will inevitably find all my truth half poisoned with deceit. This is the terrible thing about humility: that it is never fully successful. If it were only possible to be completely humble on this earth. But no, that is the trouble: You, Lord, were humble. But our humility consists in being proud and knowing all about it, and being crushed by the unbearable weight of it, and to be able to do so little about it.

How stern You are in Your mercy, and yet You must be. Your mercy has to be just because Your Truth has to be True. How stern You are, nevertheless, in Your mercy: for the more we struggle to be true, the more we discover our falsity. Is it merciful of Your light to bring us, inexorably, to despair?

No—it is not to despair that You bring me but to humility. For true humility is, in a way, a very real despair: despair of myself, in order that I may hope entirely in You.

What man can bear to fall into such darkness?

◈ XVI

Bells are meant to remind us that God alone is good, that we belong to Him, that we are not living for this world.

They break in upon our cares in order to remind us that all things pass away and that our preoccupations are not important.

They speak to us of our freedom, which responsibilities and transient cares make us forget.

They are the voice of our alliance with the God of heaven.

They tell us that we are His true temple. They call us to peace with Him within ourselves.

The Gospel of Mary and Martha is read at the end of the Blessing of a Church Bell in order to remind us of all these things.

The bells say: business does not matter. Rest in God and rejoice, for this world is only the figure and the promise of a world to come, and only those who are detached from transient things can possess the substance of an eternal promise.

The bells say: we have spoken for centuries from the towers of great Churches. We have spoken to the saints your fathers, in their land. We called them, as we call you, to sanctity. What is the word with which we called them?

We did not merely say, "Be good, come to Church." We did not merely say "Keep the commandments" but above all, "Christ is risen, Christ is risen!" And we said: "Come with us, God is good, salvation is not hard, His love has made it easy!" And this, our message, has always been for everyone, for those who came and for those who did not come, for our song is perfect as the Father in heaven is perfect and we pour our charity out upon all.

₰ XVII

It was necessary for Adam in Paradise to give the animals names. So too it is necessary for us to name the things that share our own silence with us, not in order to disturb their privacy or to disturb our own solitude with thoughts of them, but in order that the silence they dwell in and that dwells in them, may be concretized and identified for what it is. The beings that are in silence make silence real, for their silence is identified with their being. To name their being is to name their silence. And therefore it should be an act of reverence.

(Blessings make them more worthy of reverence.)

Prayer uses words to reverence beings in God.

Magic uses words to violate the silence and the sanctity of beings by treating them as if they could be torn away from God, possessed, and vilely abused, before the face of His silence. Magic insults His silence by making it the mask of an intruder, of a malign power that usurps the throne of God and substitutes itself for His presence. But what can substitute itself for Him Who is? Only that which is not can pretend to usurp His place. In doing so, it only affirms Him all the more clearly for if you suppress that which is not from the phrase "is not" you are left with nothing but "IS."

In the silence of God we have overcome magic by seeing through what is not there, and realizing that He Who IS, is closer to us than the "is not" that tries at all times to place itself between ourselves and Him.

His presence is present in my own presence. If I am, then He is. And in knowing that I am, if I penetrate to the depths of my own existence and my own present reality, the indefinable "am" that is myself in its deepest roots, then through this deep center I pass into the infinite "I Am" which is the very Name of the Almighty.

My knowledge of myself in silence (not by reflection on my self, but by penetration to the mystery of my true self which is beyond words and concepts because it is utterly particular) opens out into the silence and the "subjectivity" of God's own self.

The grace of Christ identifies me with the "engrafted word" (*insitum verbum*) which is Christ living in me. *Vivit in me Christus*. Identification by love leads to knowledge, recognition, intimate and obscure but vested with an inexpressible certainty known only in contemplation.

When we "know" (in the dark certitude of faith illumined by spiritual understanding) that we are sons of God in the one Son of God, then we experience something of the great mystery of our being in God and God in us. For we grasp, without knowing how, the awe-inspiring and admirable truth that God, bending over the abyss of His own inexhaustible being, has drawn us forth from Himself, and has clothed us in the light of His truth, and purified us in the fires of His love, and made us one, by the power of the Cross, with His only begotten Son. "Let us make man in our own image and likeness" (Genesis 1:26). "From the womb before the daystar have I begotten thee" (Psalm 109:3).

O great God, Father of all things, Whose infinite light is darkness to me, Whose immensity is to me as the void, You have called me forth out of yourself because You love me in yourself, and I am a transient expression of Your inexhaustible and eternal reality. I could not know You, I would be lost in this darkness, I would fall away from You into this void, if You did not hold me to Yourself in the Heart of Your only begotten Son.

Father, I love You Whom I do not know, and I embrace You Whom I do not see, and I abandon myself to You Whom I have offended, because You love in me Your only begotten Son. You see Him in me, You embrace Him in me, because He has willed to identify Himself completely with me by that love which brought Him to death, for me, on the Cross.

I come to You like Jacob in the garments of Esau, that is in the merits and the Precious Blood of Jesus Christ. And You, Father, Who have willed to be as though blind in the darkness of this great mystery which is the revelation of Your love, pass Your hands over my head, and bless me as Your only Son. You have willed to see me only in Him, but in willing this You have willed to see me more really as I am. For the sinful self is not my real self, it is not the self You have wanted for me, only the self that I have wanted for myself. And I no longer want this false self. But now Father, I come to You in your own Son's self, for it is His Sacred Heart that has taken possession of me and destroyed my sins and it is He Who presents me to You. And where? In the sanctuary of His own Heart, which is your palace and the temple where the saints adore You in Heaven.

❦ XVIII

It is necessary to name Him Whose silence I share and worship, for in His silence He also speaks my own name. He alone knows my name, in which I also know His name. For in the instant in which He calls me "my Son" I am aware of Him as "my Father." This recognition is, in me, an act, in Him a Person. The act in me is the movement of His Person, His Spirit, His Love, within me. When He moves, I move with Him, so that it is I also who move. And in my movement I both waken to know that "I am" and I cry "Abba, Father."

But since I am not my own father, it is useless for me to seek to awaken this recognition of Him by calling myself "Son" in the hollow of my own silence. My own voice is only able to rouse a dead echo when it calls out to itself. There will never be any awakening in me unless I am called out of darkness by Him Who is my light. Only He Who is Life is able to raise the dead. And unless He names me, I remain dead and my silence is the silence of death.

As soon as He speaks my name, my silence is the silence of infinite life, and I know that I *am* because my heart has opened to my Father in the echo of the eternal years.

My life is a listening, His is a speaking. My salvation is to hear and respond. For this, my life must be silent. Hence, my silence is my salvation.

The sacrifice that pleases God is the offering of my soul—and of other men's souls.

The soul is offered to Him when it is entirely attentive to Him. My silence, which takes me away from all other things, is therefore the sacrifice of all things and the offering of my soul to God. It is therefore my most pleasing sacrifice. If I can teach others to live in the same silence, I am offering Him a most pleasing sacrifice. The knowledge of God is better than holocausts (Osee 6:6).

Interior silence is impossible without mercy and without humility.

Difference between a *vocation* and a *category*. Those who fulfil their vocation to sanctity—or who are fulfilling it—are by that very fact unaccountable. They do not fit into categories. If you use a category in speaking of them you have to qualify your statement at once, as if they also belonged to some completely different category. In actual fact, they are in no category, they are peculiarly *themselves*, hence, they are not considered worthy of great love and respect in the eyes of men because their individuality is a sign that they are greatly loved by God and that He alone knows his secret, which is too precious to be revealed to men.

What we venerate in the Saints, beyond and above all that we know is this secret; the mystery of an innocence and of an identity perfectly hidden in God.

XIX

"Let us all hear together the conclusion of the discourse. *Fear God, and keep His commandments : for this is all man*" (Ecclesiastes 12:13).

Who hath searched out the wisdom of God that goeth before all things? . . .

To fear God is the fulness of wisdom, and fulness is from the fruits thereof . . .

The fear of the Lord is a crown of wisdom, filling up peace and the fruit of salvation . . .

Son, if thou desire wisdom, keep justice, and God will give her to thee . . .

Ecclesiasticus 1:3, 20, 22, 33

In the depths of our being is God Who commands us to live and to be. But we do not find Him merely by finding our own being.

In commanding us to *live*, He also commands us to live in a certain way. His decree is not only that we should live somehow but that we should live well, and ultimately that we should be perfect, by living in Him.

Thus in the depths of our being He has placed the light of conscience which tells us the law of life. Life is not life unless it conforms to this law which is the will of God. To live by this light is *all* of man, for thus man comes to live in God and by God. To extinguish this light by actions contrary to this law is to defile our nature. It makes us untrue to ourselves, and it makes God a liar: all sin does this, and it leads to idolatry, substituting falsehood for the truth of God.

A false conscience is a false god, a god which says nothing because it is dumb and which does nothing because it has no power. It is a mask through which we utter oracles to ourselves, telling ourselves false prophecies, giving ourselves whatever answer we want to hear: "Who changed the truth of God into a lie" (Romans 1:25).

The fear of the Lord is the beginning of wisdom.

Wisdom is the knowledge of Truth in its inmost reality, the experience of Truth, arrived at through the rectitude of our own soul. Wisdom knows God in ourselves and ourselves in God.

The fear which is the first step to wisdom is the fear of being untrue to God and to ourselves. It is the fear that we have lied to ourselves, that we have thrown down our lives at the feet of a false god.

But every man is a liar, for every man is a sinner. We have all been false to God. "But God is true; and every man a liar, as it is written" (Romans 3:4).

The fear of the Lord, which is the beginning of wisdom, is therefore the recognition of the "lie that is in our right hand" (Isaias 44:20).

"If we say that we have no sin, we deceive ourselves, and the truth is not in us . . . If we say that we have not sinned, we make Him a liar, and His word is not in us" (1 John 1:8,10).

Hence the beginning of wisdom is the confession of sin. This confession gains for us the mercy of God. It makes the light of His truth shine in our conscience, without which we cannot avoid sin. It brings the strength of His grace into our souls, binding the action of our wills to the truth in our intelligence.

The solution of the problem of life is life itself. Life is not attained by reasoning and analysis, but first of all by living. For until we have begun to live our prudence has no material to work on. And until we have begun to fail we have no way of working out our success.

PART TWO

THE LOVE OF
SOLITUDE

I

To love solitude and to seek it does not mean constantly travelling from one geographical possibility to another. A man becomes a solitary at the moment when, no matter what may be his external surroundings, he is suddenly aware of his own inalienable solitude and sees that he will never be anything but solitary. From that moment, solitude is not potential—it is actual.

However, actual solitude always places us squarely in the presence of an unrealized and even unrealizable possibility of "perfect solitude." But this has to be properly understood: for we lose the actuality of the solitude we already have if we try, with too great anxiety, to realize the material possibility for greater exterior solitude that always seems just out of reach. Actual solitude has, as one of its integral elements, the dissatisfaction and uncertainty that come from being face to face with an unrealized possibility. It is not a mad pursuit of possibilities—it is the humble acquiescence that stabilizes us in the presence of one enormous reality which is in one sense already possessed and in another a "possibility"—an object of hope.

It is only when the solitary dies and goes to heaven that he sees clearly that this possibility was already actualized in his life and he did not know it—for his solitude consisted above all in the "possible" possession of God, and of nothing else but God, in pure hope.

II

My Lord God, I have no idea where I am going. I do not see the road ahead of me. I cannot know for certain where it will end. Nor do I really know myself, and the fact that I think I am following your will does not mean that I am actually doing so. But I believe that the desire to please you does in fact please you. And I hope I have that desire in all that I am doing. I hope that I will never do anything apart from that desire. And I know that if I do this you will lead me by the right road, though I may know nothing about it. Therefore I will trust you always though I may seem to be lost and in the shadow of death. I will not fear, for you are ever with me, and you will never leave me to face my perils alone.

III

In our age everything has to be a "problem." Ours is a time of anxiety because we have willed it to be so. Our anxiety is not imposed on us by force from outside. We impose it on our world and upon one another from within ourselves.

Sanctity in such an age means, no doubt, travelling from the area of anxiety to the area in which there is no anxiety or perhaps it may mean learning, from God, to be without anxiety in the midst of anxiety.

Fundamentally, as Max Picard points out, it probably comes to this: living in a silence which so reconciles the contradictions within us that, although they remain within us, they cease to be a problem (of *World of Silence*, p. 66–67).

Contradictions have always existed in the

soul of man. But it is only when we prefer analysis to silence that they become a constant and insoluble problem. We are not meant to resolve all contradictions but to live with them and rise above them and see them in the light of exterior and objective values which make them trivial by comparison.

Silence, then, belongs to the substance of sanctity. In silence and hope are formed the strength of the Saints (Isaias 30:15).

When solitude was a problem, I had no solitude. When it ceased to be a problem I found I already possessed it, and could have possessed it all along. Yet still it was a problem because I knew after all that a merely subjective and inward solitude, the fruit of an effort at interiorisation, would never be enough. Solitude has to be objective and concrete. It has to be a communion in something greater than the world, as great as Being itself, in order that in its deep peace we may find God.

We put words between ourselves and things.

Even God has become another conceptual un-reality in a no-man's land of language that no longer serves as a means of communion with reality.

The solitary life, being silent, clears away the smoke-screen of words that man has laid down between his mind and things. In solitude we remain face to face with the naked being of things. And yet we find that the nakedness of reality which we have feared, is neither a matter of terror nor for shame. It is clothed in the friendly communion of silence, and this silence is related to love. The world our words have attempted to classify, to control and even to despise (because they could not contain it) comes close to us, for silence teaches us to know reality by respecting it where words have defiled it.

When we have lived long enough alone with the reality around us, our veneration will learn how to bring forth a few good words about it from the silence which is the mother of Truth.

Words stand between silence and silence: between the silence of things and the silence of our own being. Between the silence of the world and the silence of God. When we have really met and known the world in silence, words do not separate us from the world nor from other men, nor from God, nor from ourselves because we no longer trust entirely in language to contain reality.

Truth rises from the silence of being to the quiet tremendous presence of the Word. Then, sinking again into silence, the truth of words bears us down into the silence of God.

Or rather God rises up out of the sea like a treasure in the waves, and when language recedes His brightness remains on the shores of our own being.

IV

A man knows when he has found his vocation when he stops thinking about how to live and begins to live. Thus, if one is called to be a solitary, he will stop wondering how he is to live and start living peacefully only when he is in solitude. But if one is not called to a solitary life, the more he is alone the more will he worry about living and forget to live. When we are not living up to our true vocation, thought deadens our life, or substitutes itself for life, or gives in to life so that our life drowns out our thinking and stifles the voice of conscience. When we find our vocation—thought and life are one.

Suppose one has found completeness in his true vocation. Now everything is in unity, in order, at peace. Now work no longer interferes with prayer or prayer with work. Now contemplation no longer needs to be a special "state" that removes one from the ordinary things going on around him for God penetrates all. One does not have to think of giving an account of oneself to anyone but Him.

V

It is necessary that we find the silence of God not only in ourselves but also in one another. Unless some other man speaks to us in words that spring from God and communicate with the silence of God in our souls, we remain isolated in our own silence, from which God tends to withdraw. For inner silence depends on a continual seeking, a continual crying in the night, a repeated bending over the abyss. If we cling to a silence we think we have found forever, we stop seeking God and the silence goes dead within us. A silence in which He is no longer sought ceases to speak to us of Him. A silence from which He does not seem to be absent, dangerously threatens His continued presence. For He is found when He is sought and when He is no longer sought He escapes us. He is heard only when we hope to hear Him, and if, thinking our hope to be fulfilled, we cease to listen, He ceases to speak, His silence ceases to be vivid and becomes dead, even though we recharge it with the echo of our own emotional noise.

VI

Lord, my heart is not exalted (Psalms 130:1).

Both pride and humility seek interior silence. Pride, by a forced immobility, seeks to imitate the silence of God. But the silence of God is the perfection of Pure Life and the silence of pride is the silence of death.

Humility seeks silence not in inactivity but in ordered activity, in the activity that is proper to our poverty and helplessness before God. Humility goes to pray and finds silence through words. But because it is natural for us to pass from words to silence, and from silence to words, humility is in all things silent. Even when it speaks, humility listens. The words of humility are so simple, so gentle and so poor that they find their way without effort to the silence of God. Indeed, they are the echo of His silence, and as soon as they are spoken His silence is already present in them.

Pride is afraid to go out of itself, for fear of losing what it has produced within itself. The silence of pride is therefore menaced by the action of charity. But since humility finds nothing within itself (for humility is its own silence), it cannot lose in peace and silence by going out to listen to others or to speak to them for the love of God. In all things humility is silent and at rest and even the labor of humility is rest. *In omnibus requiem quaesivi.*

It is not speaking that breaks our silence, but the anxiety to be heard. The words of the proud man impose silence on all others, so that he alone may be heard. The humble man speaks only in order to be spoken to. The humble man asks nothing but an alms, then waits and listens.

Silence is ordered to the ultimate summing up in words of all we have lived for. We receive Christ by hearing in the word of faith. We work out our salvation in silence and hope, but sooner or later comes the time when we must confess Him openly before men, then before all the inhabitants of heaven and earth.

If our life is poured out in useless words, we will never hear anything, will never become anything, and in the end, because we have said everything before we had anything to say, we shall be left speechless at the moment of our greatest decision.

But silence is ordered to that final utterance. It is not an end in itself. Our whole life is a meditation of our last decision—the only decision that matters. And we meditate in silence. Yet we are bound to some extent, to speak to others, to help them see their way to their own decision, to teach them Christ. In teaching them Christ, our very words teach them a new silence: the silence of the Resurrection. In that silence they are formed and prepared so that they also may speak what they have heard. *I have believed, therefore have I spoken* (Psalms 115:1).

VII

When I am liberated by silence, when I am no longer involved in the measurement of life, but in the living of it, I can discover a form of prayer in which there is effectively, no distraction. My whole life becomes a prayer. My whole silence is full of prayer. The world of silence in which I am immersed contributes to my prayer.

The unity which is the work of poverty in solitude draws together all the wounds of the soul and closes them. As long as we remain poor, as long as we are empty and interested in nothing but God, we cannot be distracted. For our very poverty prevents us from being "pulled apart" (dis-tracted).

If the light that is in thee be darkness . . .

Suppose that my "poverty" be a secret hunger for spiritual riches: suppose that by pretending to empty myself, pretending to be silent, I am really trying to cajole God into enriching me with some experience—what then? Then everything becomes a distraction. All created things interfere with my quest for some special experience. I must shut them out, or they will tear me apart. What is worse—I myself am a distraction. But, unhappiest thing of all—if my prayer is centered in myself, if it seeks only an enrichment of my own self, my prayer itself will be my greatest potential distraction. Full of my own curiosity, I have eaten of the tree of Knowledge and torn myself away from myself and from God. I am left rich and alone and nothing can assuage my hunger: everything I touch turns into a distraction.

Let me seek, then, the gift of silence, and poverty, and solitude, where everything I touch is turned into prayer: where the sky is my prayer, the birds are my prayer, the wind in the trees is my prayer, for God is all in all.

For this to be so I must be really poor. I must seek nothing: but I must be most content with whatever I have from God. True poverty is that of the beggar who is glad to receive alms from anyone, but especially from God. False poverty is that of a man who pretends to have the self-sufficiency of an angel. True poverty, then, is a receiving and giving of thanks, only keeping what we need to consume. False poverty pretends not to need, pretends not to ask, strives to seek everything and refuses gratitude for anything at all.

 VIII

"*If therefore they shall say to you: Behold He is in the desert, go ye not out; behold He is in the closets, believe it not. For as lightning cometh out of the east and appeareth even into the west, so shall the coming of the Son of Man be*" (Matthew 24:26–28).

Christ, Who will come unexpectedly at the end of time—and no one can guess the moment of His coming—comes also to those who are His own at every moment of time, and they cannot see or guess His coming. Yet where He is, there they are. Like eagles, they gather by instinct, not knowing how, and they find Him at every moment.

Just as there is no way of saying with certainty where and when He will appear at the end of the world, so too there is no way of saying with certainty where and when He will manifest Himself to contemplative souls.

There are many who have sought Him in the desert and have not found Him there and there are many who have hidden themselves with Him in reclusion and He has refused Himself to them. To catch Him is as easy as catching the lightning. And like lightning, He strikes where He pleases.

All truly contemplative souls have this in common: not that they gather exclusively in the desert, or that they shut themselves up in reclusion, but that where He is, there they are. And how do they find Him? By technique? There is no technique for finding Him. They find Him by *His will*. And His will, bringing them grace within and arranging their lives exteriorly, carries them infallibly to the precise place in which they can find Him. Even there they do not know how they have got there, or what they are really doing.

As soon as a man is fully disposed to be alone with God, he is alone with God no matter where he may be—in the country, the monastery, the woods or the city. The lightning flashes from east to west, illuminating the whole horizon and striking where it pleases and at the same instant the infinite liberty of God flashes in the depths of that man's soul, and he is illumined. At that moment he sees that though he seems to be in the middle of his journey, he has already arrived at the end. For the life of grace on earth is the beginning of the life of glory. Although he is a traveller in time, he has opened his eyes, for a moment, in eternity.

IX

It is a greater thing and a better prayer to live in Him Who is Infinite, and to rejoice that He is Infinite, than to strive always to press His infinity into the narrow space of our own hearts. As long as I am content to know that He is infinitely greater than I, and that I cannot know Him unless He shows Himself to me, I will have Peace, and He will be near me and in me, and I will rest in Him. But as soon as I desire to know and enjoy Him for myself, I reach out to do violence to Him Who evades me, and in so doing I do violence to myself and fall back upon myself in sorrow and anxiety, knowing that He has gone His way.

In true prayer, although every silent moment

remains the same, every moment is a new discovery of a new silence, a new penetration into that eternity in which all things are always new. We know, by fresh discovery, the deep reality that is our concrete existence here and now and in the depths of that reality we receive from the Father light, truth, wisdom and peace. These are the reflection of God in our souls which are made to His image and likeness.

X

Let this be my only consolation, that wherever I am You, my Lord, are loved and praised.

The trees indeed love You without knowing You. The tiger lilies and corn flowers are there, proclaiming that they love You, without being aware of Your presence. The beautiful dark clouds ride slowly across the sky musing on You like children who do not know what they are dreaming of, as they play.

But in the midst of them all, I know You, and I know of Your presence. In them and in me I know of the love which they do not know, and, what is greater, I am abashed by the presence of Your love in me. O kind and terrible love, which You have given me, and which could never be in my heart if You did not love me! For in the midst of these beings which have never offended You, I am loved by You, and it would seem most of all as one who has offended You. I am seen by You under the sky, and my offenses have been forgotten by You—but I have not forgotten them.

Only one thing I ask: that the memory of them should not make me afraid to receive into my heart the gift of Love—which You have placed in me. I will receive it because I am unworthy. In doing so I will only love You all the more, and give Your mercy greater glory.

Remembering that I have been a sinner, I will love You in spite of what I have been, knowing that my love is precious because it is Yours, rather than my own. Precious to You because it comes from Your own Son, but precious even more because it makes me Your son.

XI

Vocation to Solitude—To deliver oneself up, to hand oneself over, entrust oneself completely to the silence of a wide landscape of woods and hills, or sea, or desert; to sit still while the sun comes up over that land and fills its silences with light. To pray and work in the morning and to labor and rest in the afternoon, and to sit still again in meditation in the evening when night falls upon that land and when the silence fills itself with darkness and with stars. This is a true and special vocation. There are few who are willing to belong completely to such silence, to let it soak into their bones, to breathe nothing but silence, to feed on silence, and to turn the very substance of their life into a living and vigilant silence.

The martyr is a man who has made a decision strong enough to be proved by death.

The solitary is a man who has made a decision strong enough to be proved by the wilderness: that is to say, by death. For the wilderness is full of uncertainty and peril and humiliation and fear, and the solitary lives all day long in the face of death. Hence it is clear that the solitary is the martyr's younger brother. It is the Holy Spirit Himself Who makes the decision that segregates martyrs and solitaries in Christ.

The vocation to martyrdom is charismatic and extraordinary. So too in a sense is the vocation to solitude. We do not become martyrs by any human plan, and we do not become solitaries by any mere design of our own. Even the desire for solitude must be supernatural if it is to be effective and if it is supernatural it will probably also be a contradiction of many of our own plans and desires. We may indeed look ahead and foresee and desire the path that leads us to the desert, but in the end, solitaries are made by God and not by man.

No matter whether we be called to community or to solitude, our vocation is to build upon the foundation of the Apostles and the prophets, and on the chief cornerstone which is Christ. This means that we are called to fulfil and to realize the great mystery of His power in us, the power that raised Him from the dead and called us from the ends of the earth to live, to the Father, in Him. Whatever may be our vocation we are called to be witnesses and ministers of the Divine Mercy.

The Christian solitary does not seek solitude merely as an atmosphere or as a setting for a special and exalted spirituality. Nor does he seek solitude as a favorable means for obtaining something he wants—contemplation. He seeks solitude as an expression of his total gift of himself to God. His solitude is not a means of getting something, but a gift of himself. As such, it may imply renouncement and contempt of "the world" in its bad sense. It is never a renunciation of the Christian community. Indeed, it may express the solitary's conviction that he is not good enough for most of the visible exercises of the community, that his own part is to carry out some hidden function, in the community's spiritual cellar.

XII

The solitary life is above all a life of prayer.

We do not pray for the sake of praying, but for the sake of being heard. We do not pray in order to listen to ourselves praying but in order that God may hear us and answer us. Also, we do not pray in order to receive just *any* answer: it must be God's answer.

Therefore a solitary will be a man who is always praying, and who there is always intent upon God, solicitous for the purity of his own prayer to God, careful not to substitute his own answers for God's answers, careful not to make prayer an end in itself, careful to keep his prayer hidden and simple and clean. In so doing, he can mercifully forget that his "perfection" depends on his prayer: he can forget himself and live in expectation of God's answers.

It seems to me that this is not quite comprehensible if we forget that the life of prayer is founded on prayer of *petition*—no matter what it may develop into later on.

Far from ruining the purity of solitary prayer, petition guards and preserves that purity. The solitary, more than anyone else, is always aware of his poverty and of his needs before God. Since he depends directly on God for everything material and spiritual, he has to ask for everything. His prayer is an expression of his poverty. Petition, for him, can hardly become a mere formality, a concession to human custom, as if he did not need God in everything.

The solitary, being a man of prayer, will come to know God by knowing that his prayer is *always answered*. From there, he can go on, if God wills, to contemplation.

Gratitude is therefore the heart of the solitary life, as it is the heart of the Christian life.

From his first day in solitude, the hermit

should set his heart upon understanding how to afflict his whole being with tears and desire before God. Then he will be like Daniel, to whom the angel brought God's answer (cf Daniel 10: 12). "Fear not, Daniel: for from the first day that thou didst set thy heart *to understand, to afflict thyself* in the sight of thy God, thy words have been heard . . ."

Qualities of prayer:

1. Unhesitating faith (Matthew 21:21; James 1:6), which depends on "singleness" of mind and purpose.

2. Persevering confidence (Luke 11).

 XIII

It seems to me that the solitary contemplative life is an imitation and fulfilment in ourselves of these words of Jesus: "The Son can do nothing of himself, but only what He sees the Father doing. For whatever he does, this the Son also does in like manner. For the Father loves the Son and shows him all that he himself does" (John 5:19–20).

This imitation consists in being and acting in the same relation to Jesus as Jesus to the Father. (John 5:24). "He who hears my word, and believes him who sent me, has life everlasting . . ." The Father draws us to Jesus (John 6:37; 6:44–45). "Everyone who has listened to the Father, and has learned, comes to me." We listen to the Father best in solitude. Jesus is the Bread of Life given to us in solitude (John 6:58). "As the living Father has sent me, and as I live because of the Father, so he who eats me, he also shall live because of me."

The solitary life then is the life of one drawn by the Father into the wilderness there to be nourished by no other spiritual food than Jesus. For in Jesus the Father gives Himself to us and nourishes us with His own inexhaustible life. The life of solitude therefore must be a continual communion and thanksgiving in which we behold by faith all that goes on in the depths of God, and lose our taste for any other life or any other spiritual food.

Also it seems to me that the solitary life fulfils the above texts by the abandonment of the Psalmist: "But I am a beggar and poor: *the Lord is careful for me*" (39:18). We live in constant dependence upon this merciful kindness of the Father, and thus our whole life is a life of gratitude—a constant response to His help which comes to us at every moment. I think every one finds this out in any vocation, provided it is his true vocation.

The solitary life is a life in which we cast our care upon the Lord and delight only in the help that comes from Him. Whatever He does is our joy. We reproduce His goodness in us by our gratitude. (Or—our gratitude is the reflection of His mercy. It is what makes us like Him.)

The truly solitary life has a completely different character from the partial solitude which can be enjoyed from time to time in the intervals allowed by social living. When we receive our solitude by intervals, we taste its value by contrast with another value. When we really live alone, there is no contrast.

I must not go into solitude to immobilize my life, to reduce all things to a frozen concentration upon some inner experience. When solitude alternates with common living, it can take on this character of a halt, of a moment of stillness, an interval of concentration. Where solitude is not an interval but a continuous whole, we may well renounce altogether the sense of concentration and the feeling of spiritual stillness. Our whole life may flow out to meet the Being and the Silence of the days in which we are immersed, and we can work out our salvation by quiet, continued action.

It is even possible that in solitude I shall return to my beginning and rediscover the value and perfection of simple vocal prayer—and take greater joy in this than in contemplation.

So that the cenobite may have high contemplation, while the hermit has only his *Pater* and *Ave Maria*. In that event I choose the life of a hermit in which I live in God *always*, speaking to Him with simplicity, rather than a life of disjointed activity sublimated by a few moments of fire and exaltation.

The solitary is necessarily a man who does what he wants to do. In fact, he has nothing else to do. That is why his vocation is both dangerous and despised. Dangerous because, in fact, he must become a saint by doing what he wants to do, instead of doing what he does not want to do. It is very hard to be a saint by doing what you like. It means that what you like is always God's will. It means therefore that you are not likely to like what is not God's will, and that God Himself will cover your mistaken choices by accepting them, in good part, as "His will."

This vocation is wisely despised by those who fear to do what they want to do, knowing well that what they want to do is not the will of God. But the Solitary must be a man who has the courage to do the thing he most wants in the world to do—to live in solitude. It requires heroic humility and heroic hope—the mad hope that God will protect him against himself, that God loves him so much that He will accept such a choice as if it were His own. Such hope is a sign that the choice of solitude is God's choice. That the desire for solitude is possibly a divine vocation. That it implies the grace to please God by making our own decisions in the humiliating uncertainty of an everlasting silence that never approves or disapproves a single choice we make.

I should be able to return to solitude each time as to the place I have never described to anybody, as the place which I have never brought anyone to see, as the place whose silence has mothered an interior life known to no one but God alone.

 XIV

You pray best when the mirror of your soul is empty of every image except the Image of the Invisible Father. This image is the Wisdom of the Father, the Word of the Father, *Verbum spirans amorem*, the glory of the Father.

We glorify the Father in hope, through the darkness of His image, which excludes every other likeness from our soul, making us live by a pure relationship and dependence on the Father. This life of dependence, perfected in pure faith, is the only life which accords with our sacramental character of sons of the Father in Christ.

Excluding images.

Only pure love can empty the soul perfectly

of the images of created things and elevate you above desire.

In disposing ourselves for this we need not attempt, by ourselves, the vain task of emptying ourselves of every image: we must first begin by replacing harmful images by good ones, then by renouncing even our good images that are useless or which involve us uselessly in passion and emotion. Landscape is a good liberator from all such images, for it calms and pacifies the imagination and the emotions and leaves the will free to seek God in faith.

The delicate action of grace in the soul is profoundly disturbed by all human violence. Passion, when it is inordinate, does violence to the spirit and its most dangerous violence is that in which we seem to find peace. Violence is not completely fatal until it ceases to disturb us.

The peace produced by grace is a spiritual stability too deep for violence—it is unshakeable, unless we ourselves admit the power of passion into our own sanctuary. Emotion can trouble the surface of our being, but it will not stir the depths if these are held and possessed by grace.

Spiritual violence is most dangerous when it is most spiritual—that is, least emotional. Violence which acts in the depths of the will without any surface upheaval carries our whole being into captivity with no apparent struggle. Such is the violence of deliberate and unresisted sin which seems to be not violence but peace.

There is also a violence of consented inordinate desire, which is not generally sinful, but which impedes the work of grace and makes it easier for charity to be driven out of us altogether. Such consent involves us too deeply in the decisions of passion, and yet it may do so under the pretext of serving God. The most dangerous spiritual violence is that which carries our will away with a false enthusiasm which seems to come from God but which is in reality inspired by passion.

Many of our most cherished plans for the glory of God are only inordinate passion in disguise. And the proof of this is found in the excitement which they produce. The God of peace is never glorified by violence.

There is only one kind of violence which cap-

XV

As soon as you are really alone you are with God.

Some people live for God, some live with God, some live in God.

Those who live for God, live with other people and live in the activities of their community. Their life is what they *do*.

Those who live with God also live for Him, but they do not live in what they do for Him, they live in what they are before Him. Their life is to reflect Him by their own simplicity and by the perfection of His being reflected in their poverty.

Those who live in God do not live with other men or in themselves still less in what they do, for He does all things in them.

Sitting under this same tree I can live for God, or with Him, or in Him.

If I were writing this *for* Him, it would not be enough.

To live with Him it is necessary to refrain constantly from speech and to moderate our desires of communication with men, even about God.

Yet it is not hard to commune at the same time with other men and with Him, as long as we find them in Him.

Solitary life—essentially the most simple. Common life prepares for it in so far as we *find God* in the simplicity of common life—then seek Him more and find Him better in the *greater simplicity* of solitude.

But if our community life is intensely complicated—(through our own fault)—we are likely to become even more complicated in solitude.

Do not flee to solitude from the community. Find God first in the community, then He will lead you to solitude.

A man cannot understand the true value of silence unless he has a real respect for the validity of language: for the reality which is expressible in language is found, face to face and without medium, in silence. Nor would we find this reality in itself, that is to say in its own silence, unless we were first brought there by language.

Words in the Gospel:

1) Jesus *fulfils the words* of the prophets (John 12:32 and Moses especially John 5:47). His miracles were "words"—they did not believe words. "Who hath believed our report?" (Isaias 53:1). Jesus' *words* will judge the world (John 12:41; John 15:22).

2) The words of Jesus are the words of the Father (John 12:49; John 17:8).

3) His words *sanctify* us (John 15:3).

4) Especially in so far as they are or imply precepts which keep us in His love (John 15:10-11-12) and bring us through Him to the Father (John 17:6–10).

Words in Genesis (Genesis 2:19–20). Adam

☒ XVI

We find God in our own being which is the mirror of God.

But how do we find our being?

Actions are the doors and windows of being. Unless we act we have no way of knowing what we are. And the experience of our existence is impossible without some experience of knowing or some experience of experience.

Hence we cannot find the depths of our being by renouncing all activity.

If we renounce spiritual activity, we can relapse into a certain darkness and peace, but it is the darkness and peace of the flesh.

We feel that we are, but the being which we experience is the being of the flesh only and if we sleep in this darkness and fall in love with its sweetness we will wake up to perform the works of the flesh.

Hence to find our spiritual being we must travel down the path made by our spiritual activity.

But when we act according to grace, our actions are not ours alone, they belong to God. If we follow them to their source, we will become at least potentially capable of an experience of God. For His actions in us reveal His being in us.

The whole of life is to spiritualize our activities by humility and faith, to silence our nature by charity.

"To go out of ourselves" is to act at the very summit of our being, not moved by our own nature but moved by God Who is at once infinitely above us and Who yet dwells in the depths of our being.

To rest from this action—I mean to taste the fruit of this action—is to rest in the being of God above our own being—Where your treasure is there your heart is also. You appreciate that all the values (treasure) of your spiritual act come from God—and your heart rests in the source from which all that is good in you comes. You do not possess your being in yourself but only in Him from Whom it springs.

By faith I find my own true being in God.

A perfect act of faith should, at the same time, be a perfect act of humility.

God does not tell His purest secrets to one who is prepared to reveal them. He has secrets which He tells to those who will communicate some idea of them to others. But these secrets are the common property of many. He has other secrets, which cannot be told. The mere desire to tell them makes us incapable of receiving them.

The greatest of God's secrets is God Himself.

He waits to communicate Himself to me in a way that I can never express to others or even think about coherently to myself. I must desire it in silence. It is for this that I must leave all things.

XVII

The great work of the solitary life is gratitude. The hermit is one who knows the mercy of God better than other men because his whole life is one of complete dependence, in silence and in hope, upon the hidden mercy of our Heavenly Father.

The further I advance into solitude the more clearly I see the goodness of all things.

In order to live happily in solitude I must have a compassionate knowledge of the goodness of other men, a reverent knowledge of the goodness of all creation and a humble knowledge of the goodness of my own body and of my own soul. How can I live in solitude if I do not see everywhere the goodness of God, my Creator and Redeemer and the Father of all good?

What is it that has made me evil and hateful to myself? It is my own folly, my own darkness, which have divided me, by sin, against the light which God has placed in my soul to be the reflection of His goodness and the witness of His mercy.

Shall I drive evil out of my soul by wrestling with my own darkness? This is not what God has planned for me. It is sufficient to turn away from my darkness to His light. I do not have to run away from myself; it is sufficient that I find myself, not as I have made myself, by my own stupidity, but as He has made me in His wisdom and remade me in His infinite mercy. For it is His will that my body and soul should be the Temple of His Holy Spirit, that my life should reflect the radiance of His love and my whole being repose in His peace. Then will I truly know Him, since I am in Him and He is truly in me.

XVIII

The Psalms are the true garden of the solitary and the Scriptures are his Paradise. They reveal their secrets to him because, in his extreme poverty and humility, he has nothing else to live by except their fruits. For the true solitary the reading of Scripture ceases to be an "exercise" among other exercises, a means of "cultivating" the intellect or "the spiritual life" or "appreciating the liturgy." To those who read Scripture in an academic or aesthetic or merely devotional way the Bible indeed offers pleasant refreshment and profitable thoughts. But to learn the inner secrets of the Scriptures we must make them our true daily bread, find God in them when we are in greatest need—and usually when we can find

Him nowhere else and have nowhere else to look!

In solitude I have at last discovered that You have desired the love of my heart, O my God, the love of my heart as it is—the love of a man's heart.

I have found and have known, by Your great mercy, that the love of a man's heart that is abandoned and broken and poor is most pleasing to You and attracts the gaze of Your pity, and that it is Your desire and Your consolation, O my Lord, to be very close to those who love You and call upon You as their Father. That You have perhaps no greater "consolation" (if I may so speak) than to console Your afflicted children and those who came to You poor and empty-handed with nothing but their humanness and their limitations and great trust in Your mercy.

Only solitude has taught me that I do not have to be a god or an angel to be pleasing to You, that I do not have to become a pure intelligence without feeling and without human imperfection before You will listen to my voice.

You do not wait for me to become great before You will be with me and hear me and answer me. It is my lowliness and my humanness that have drawn You to make me Your equal by condescending to my level and living in me by Your merciful care.

And now it is Your desire, not that I give You the thanks and recognition You receive from Your great angels, but the love and gratitude that comes from the heart of a child, a son of woman, Your own Son.

My Father, I know You have called me to live alone with You, and to learn that if I were not a mere man, a mere human being capable of all mistakes and all evil, also capable of a frail and errant human affection for You, I would not be capable of being Your son. You desire the love of a man's heart because Your Divine Son also loves You with a man's Heart and He became Man in order that my heart and His Heart should love You in one love, which is a human love born and moved by Your Holy Spirit.

If therefore I do not love You with a man's love and with a man's simplicity and with the humility to be myself I will never taste the full sweetness of Your Fatherly mercy, and Your Son, as far as my life goes, will have died in vain.

It is necessary that I be human and remain human in order that the Cross of Christ be not made void. Jesus died not for the angels but for men.

This is what I learn from the Psalms in solitude, for the Psalms are full of the human simplicity of men like David who knew God as men and loved Him as men, and therefore knew Him, the One true God, Who would send His only begotten Son to men in the likeness of man that they, while still remaining men, might love Him with a divine love.

And this is the mystery of our vocation: not that we cease to be men in order to become angels or gods, but that the love of my man's heart can become God's love for God and men, and my human tears can fall from my eyes as the tears of God because they well up from the motion of His Spirit in the heart of His incarnate Son. Hence—the Gift of Piety grows in solitude, nourished by the Psalms.

When this is learned, then our love of other men becomes pure and strong. We can go out to them without vanity and without complacency, loving them with something of the purity and gentleness and hiddenness of God's love for us.

This is the true fruit and the true purpose of Christian solitude.